Jaime's
Inspirations

Jaime's Inspirations

POEMS FROM
THE HEART AND MIND

Jaime P. Fidler

Copyright © 2024 by Jaime P. Fidler
All rights reserved. This book or any portion thereof may not be reproduced or used in any manner whatsoever without the express written permission of the publisher except for the use of brief quotation in a book review.

Leavitt Peak Press

ISBN: 978-1-965679-24-1 Paperback
ISBN: 978-1-965679-25-8 Ebook
Rev. date: 10/08/2024

This book is dedicated to the special people who have inspired my life in special ways at special times.

I would also like to thank from my heart Andy Mwandacha Maganga for suggesting I collect the poems I had written, which he thought were very inspirational,
into a book to share with others.

Contents

Shine ••• 1
Present Memories ••• 3
Daydream ••• 5
The Person You Love ••• 7
Gene ••• 9
Pain ••• 11
Shadow ••• 13
Sunshine ••• 15
Lost in the Illusion of Love ••• 17
Memories ••• 19
Liquid ••• 21
Love ••• 23
Love ••• 25
What is Love ••• 27
Images ••• 29
Blindness ••• 31
About the Author ••• 33

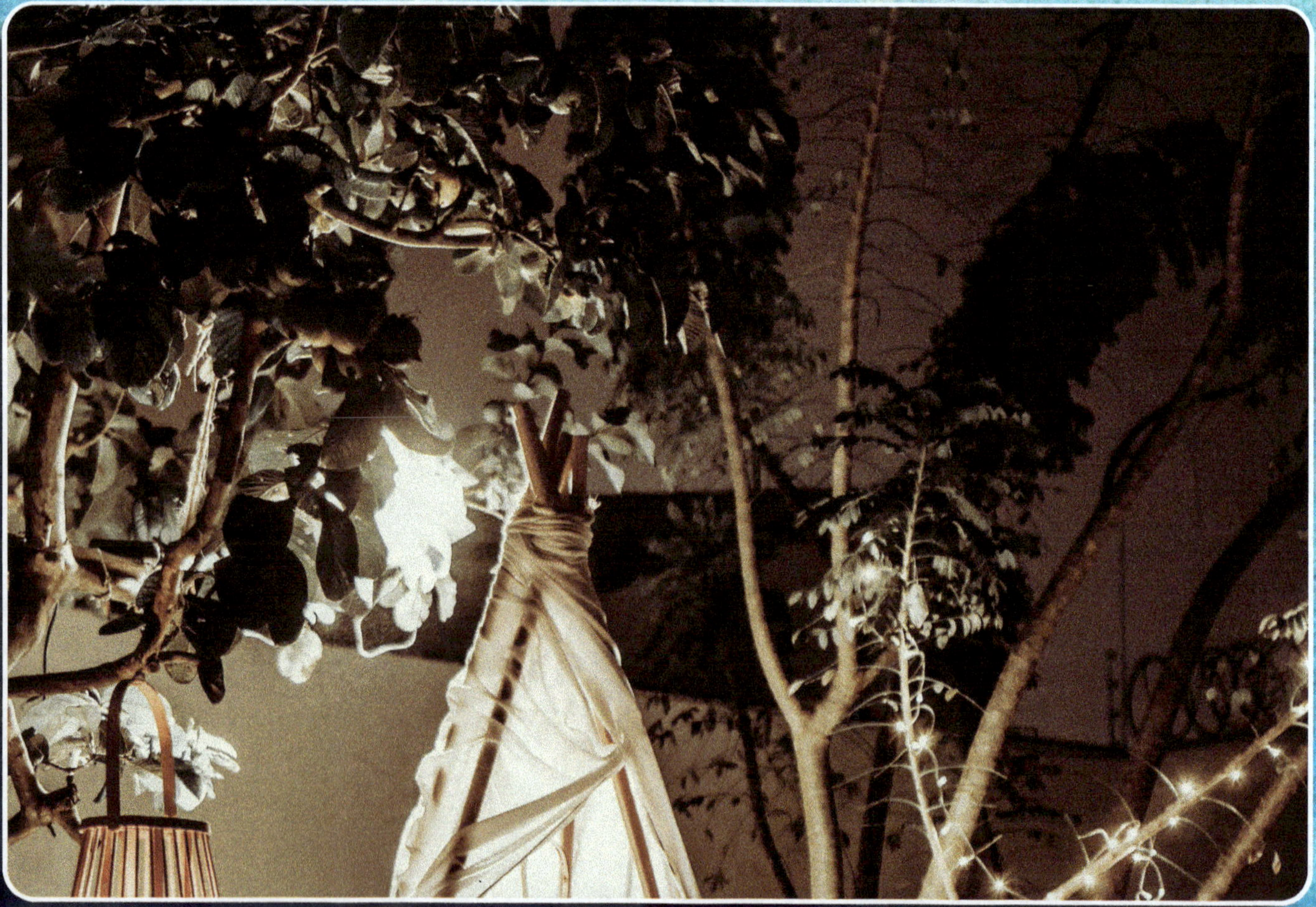

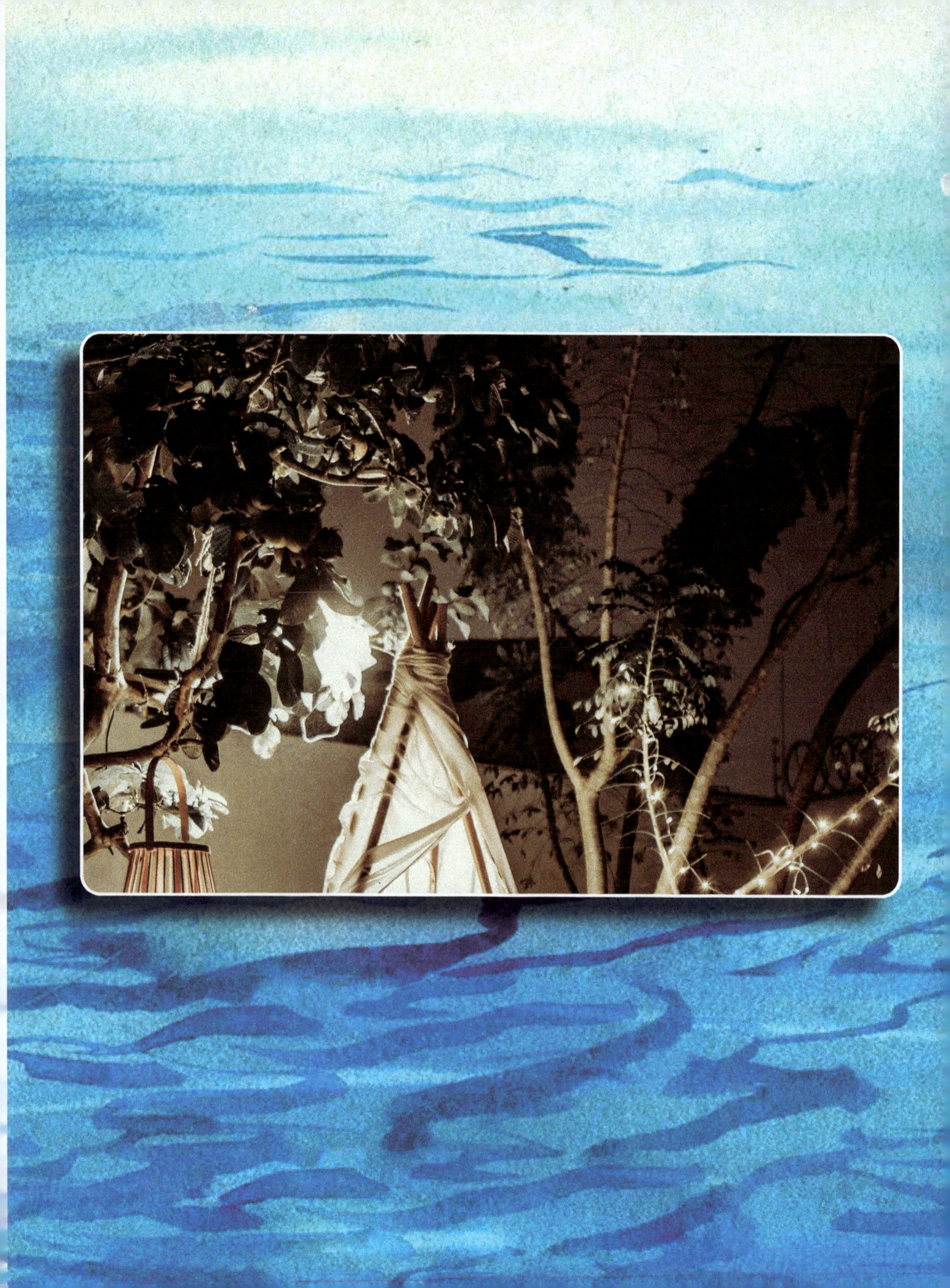

Shine

You have shone the light through my heart
You have said the words I want to keep
You have been the one I've chosen
Baby, you're the one I want to keep

I have said some words to push you away
But I want you closer to words I can't say
I'm so sorry for every word I said
To make you change and feel this way

I wish you could see my heart
Because it's pouring out tears to the one I want
Every day, every night, I dream of you
I wonder why you did what you did
To make me cry

The last time we were together
You seemed more distant than ever
The feelings I have are so hard to ignore
Can you give me one more chance
I won't act this way again ever
You're the one I love and want to keep
'Cause, baby, you've shone the light
To make me see
You are the light my shadow took
I won't give up on you that easily
I must take another look

You have shone the light through my heart
You have said the words I want to keep
You have been the one I've chosen
Baby, you're the one I want to keep

One last thing I have to say
You have to see me through all this
'Cause, baby, I want you so
Can't you see through my heart and soul
I want you and only you
Forevermore

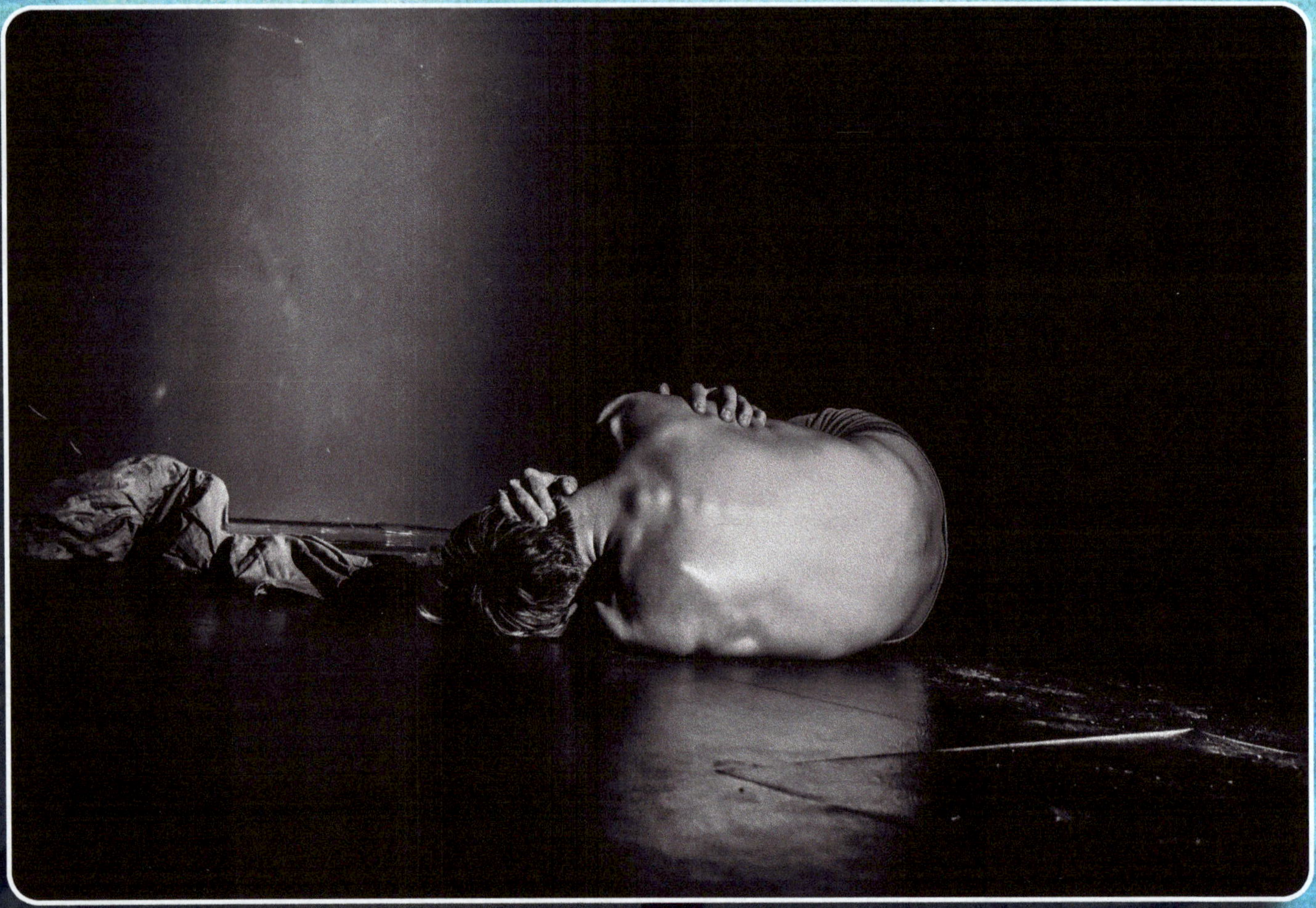

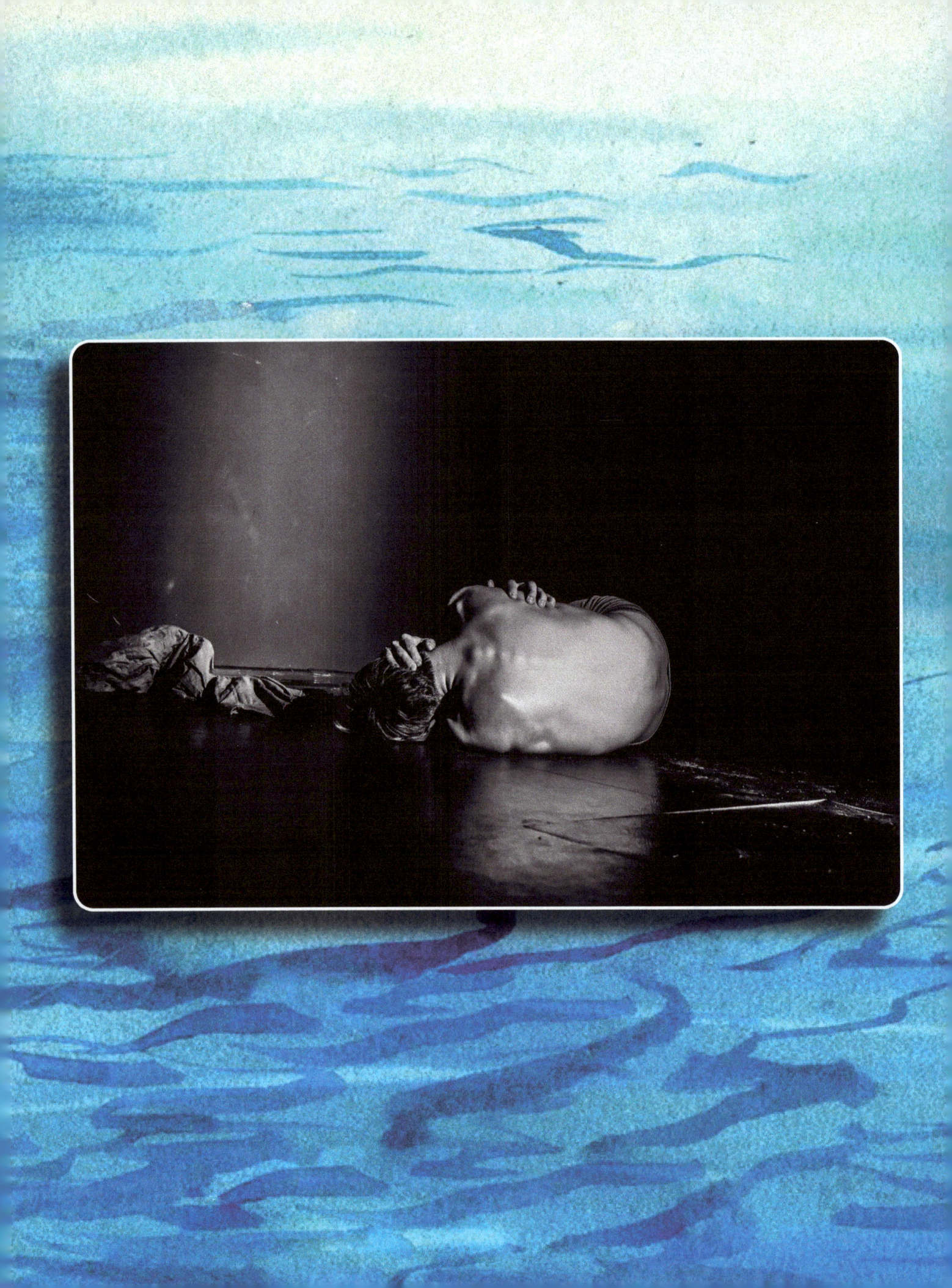

Present Memories

It hurts me as I blink
Look at myself in the mirror
It smacks me in the face
The past and the future

To the loneliness I feel
Which prison do I see
As I walk slowly
Through my memories

Walking down the aisle
To nothing at all
It hurts me inside
No one else sees it at all

To the feelings I feel
When you look upon my face
The love that I lost
The love I defaced

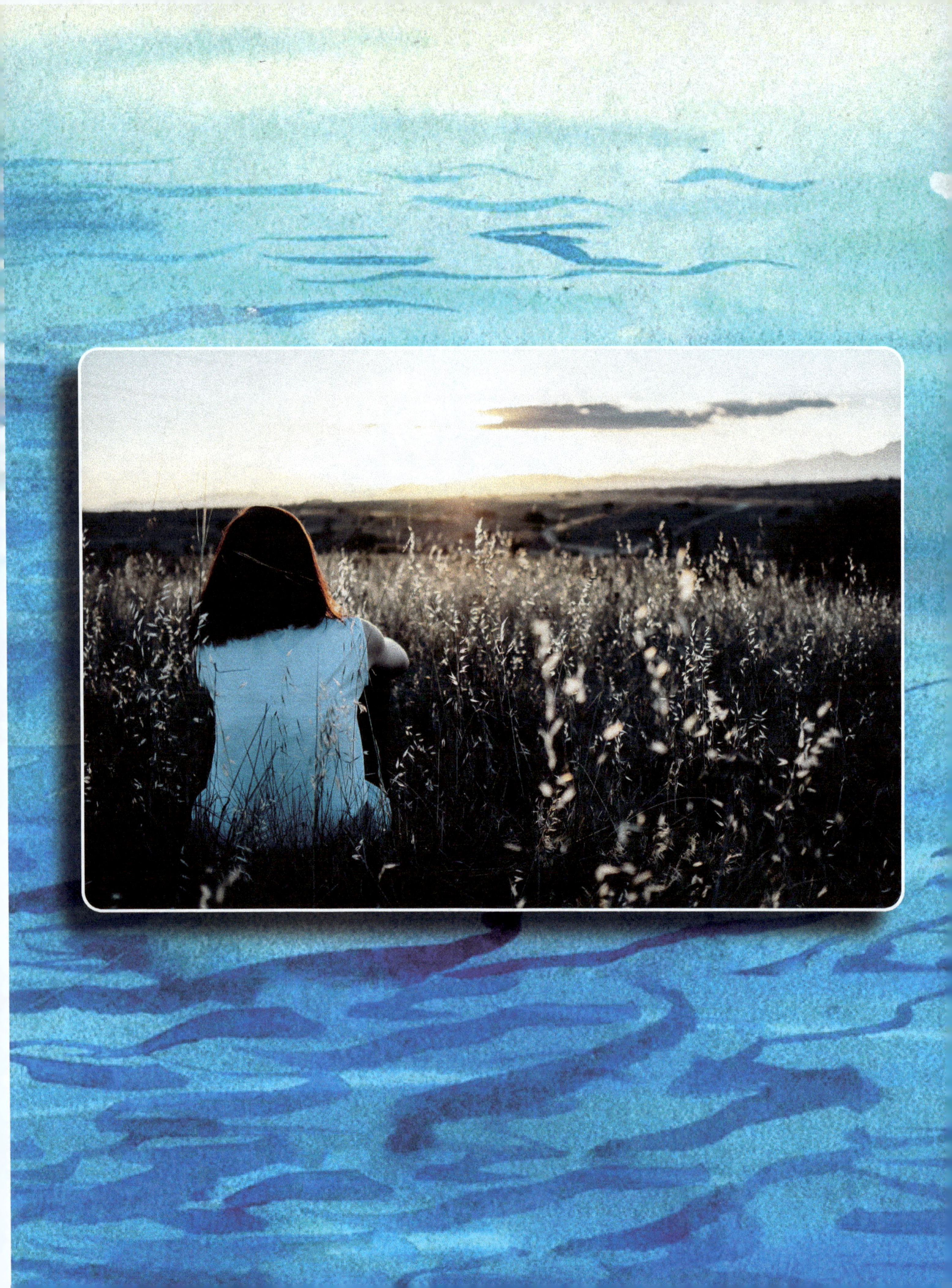

Daydream

As I look at the flames
Glowing in the dark
Charcoal underneath the wood
Smouldering red hot

To the bricks in behind
Green, blue and yellow flames
To the red hot burning
Which we both feel the same

For the heart is still sizzling
For you and me
To be with each other
For all eternity
Is it gone
One will never know
Let time pass by
Let it glow
Still in our hearts

The electrifying passion
That I still feel
Lonely as I am
You will never know
The heart I have
Is broken with tears
It's crying out
Echoing in your ears

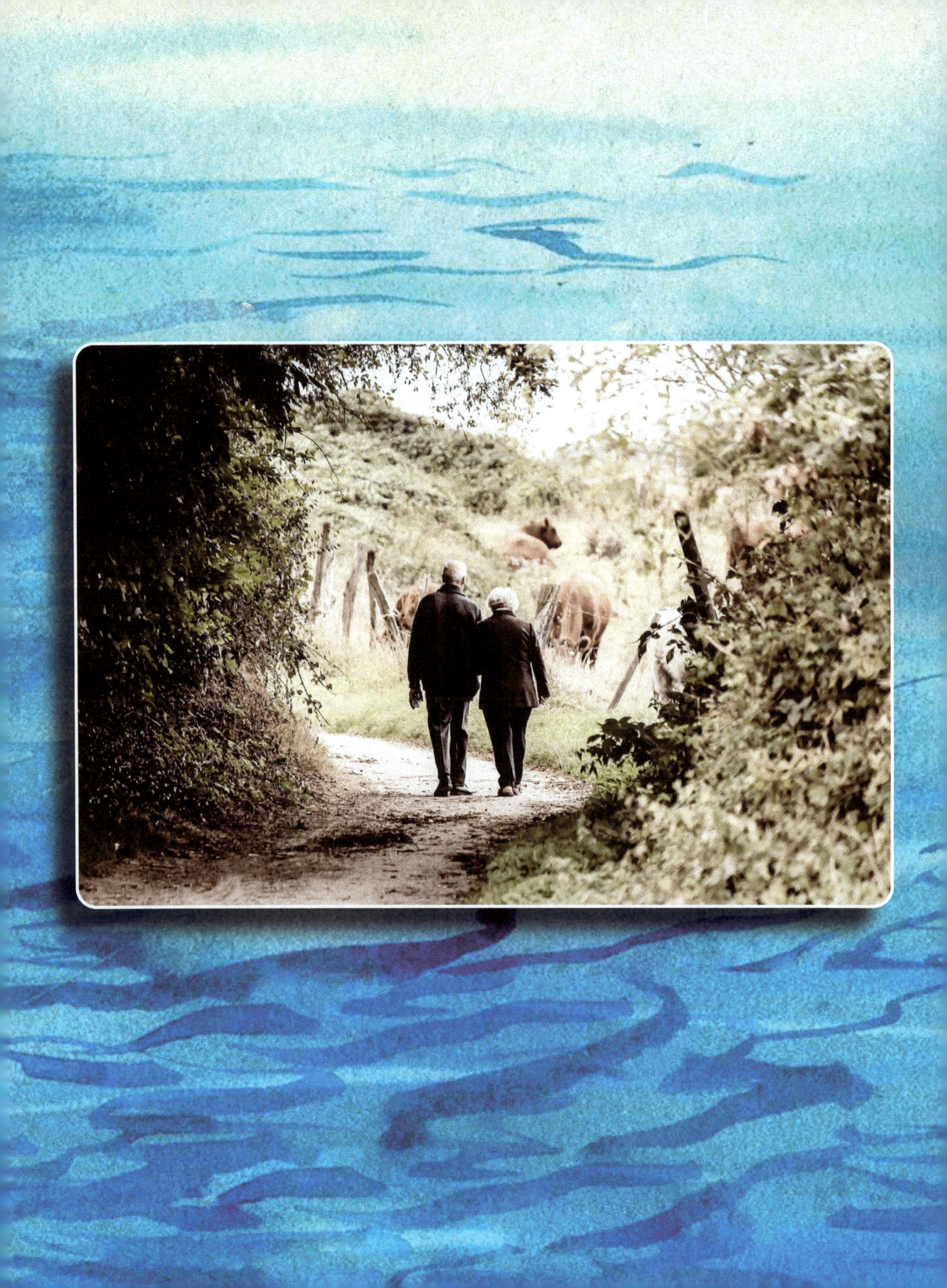

The Person You Love

The person you love
Never seems to leave
He is always there
But somehow can't share
His love
His feelings
His loving towards you
If you get a man like this
He'll be with you
The rest of your life
You can't seem to let go
'Cause you love him so much
If you find yourself like this
Don't let him go
Stay with him until you know
True love has finally ended
We go on walks in the warm, breezy air
I look into his eyes
And see the magic there
I tell him I love him
And that I care
As we walk in the warm, breezy air

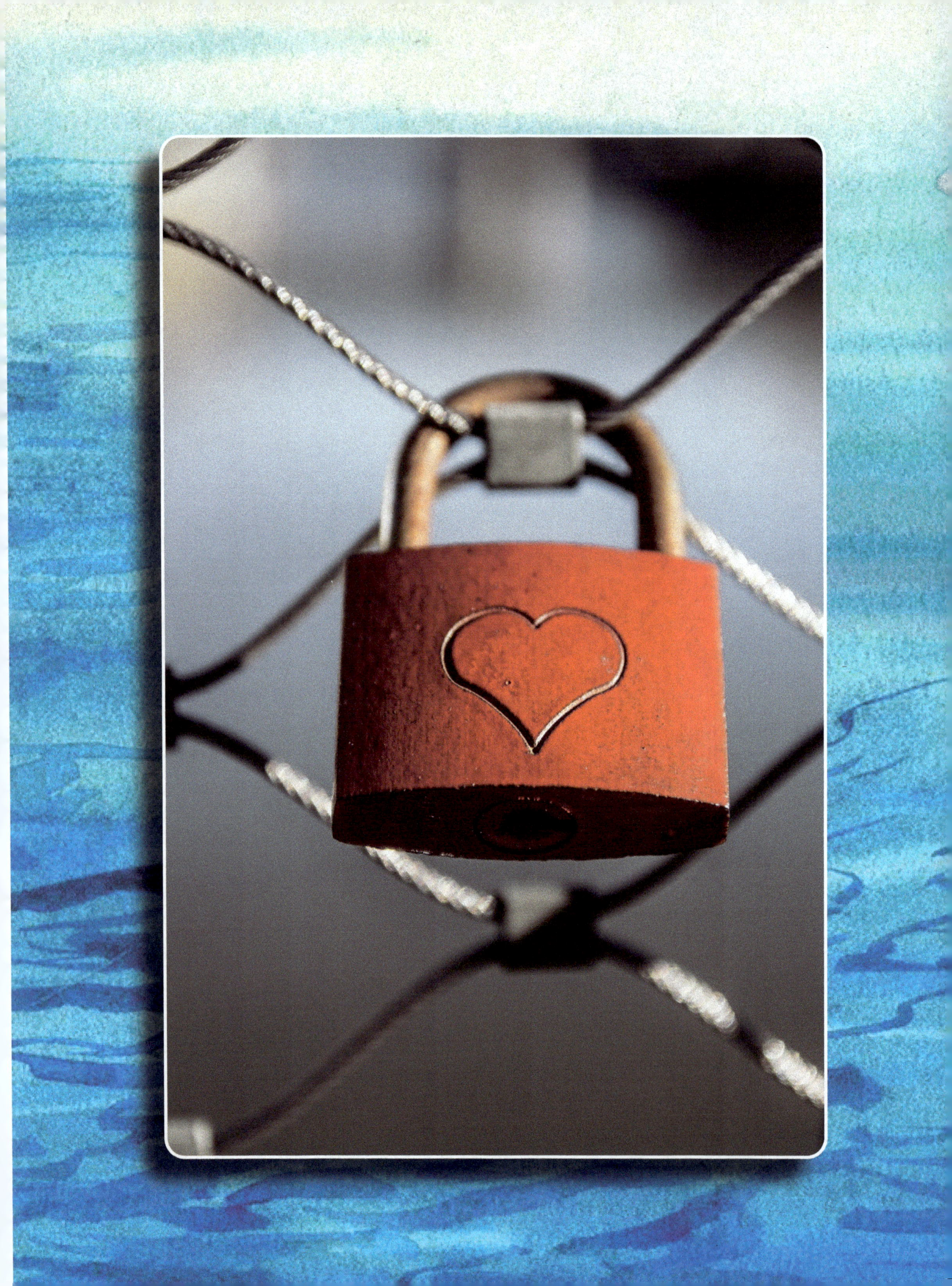

Gene

As I lay in the dark
I think about you
I wonder where
You'll end up
I wonder who
Will be the special person
You give your heart to
I hope she's kind and special
Because you deserve the best
For this Valentine's Day
And for all the rest

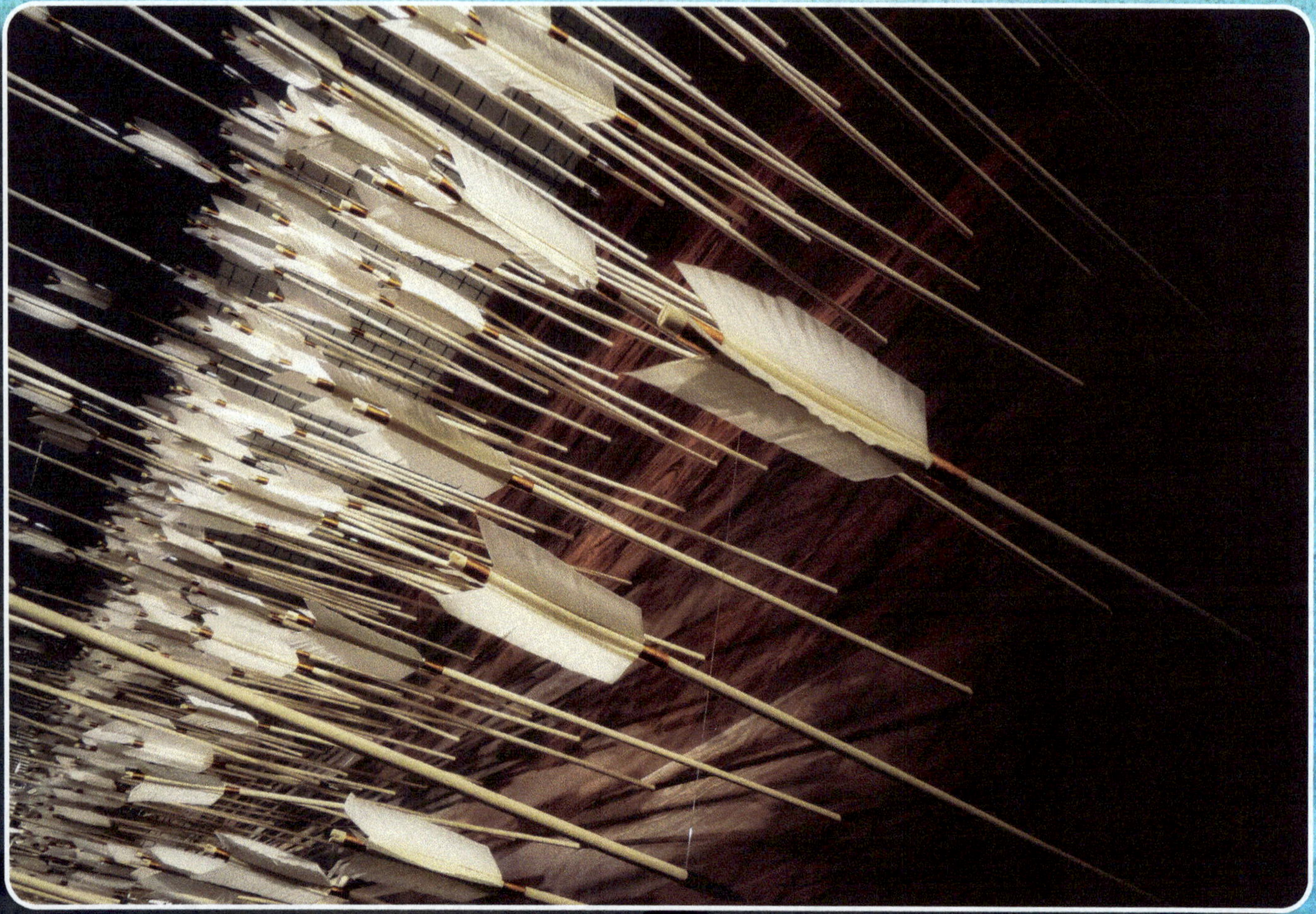

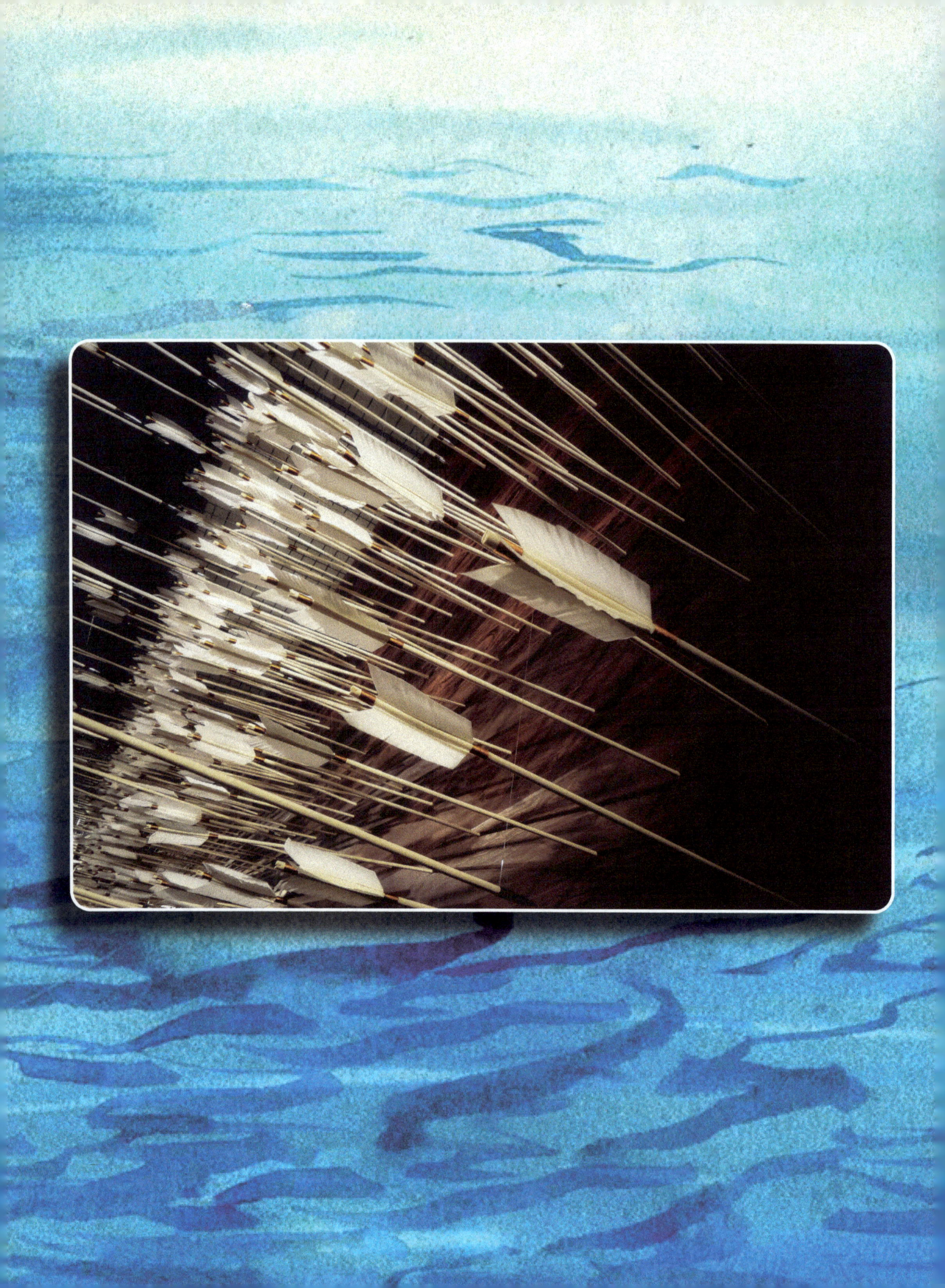

Pain

Do you ever get a pain
That you feel inside
That won't leave you
Till the day you die

It's stuck inside of me
As sharp as sharp can be
How do you get rid of this pain
That feels jagged inside
You're the one who took my hand
Swept me off my feet
You're the one who took my love
Cherished it most deeply

You're the one who holds me tight
Never lets me go
You're the one who'll be beside me
If I never let you go

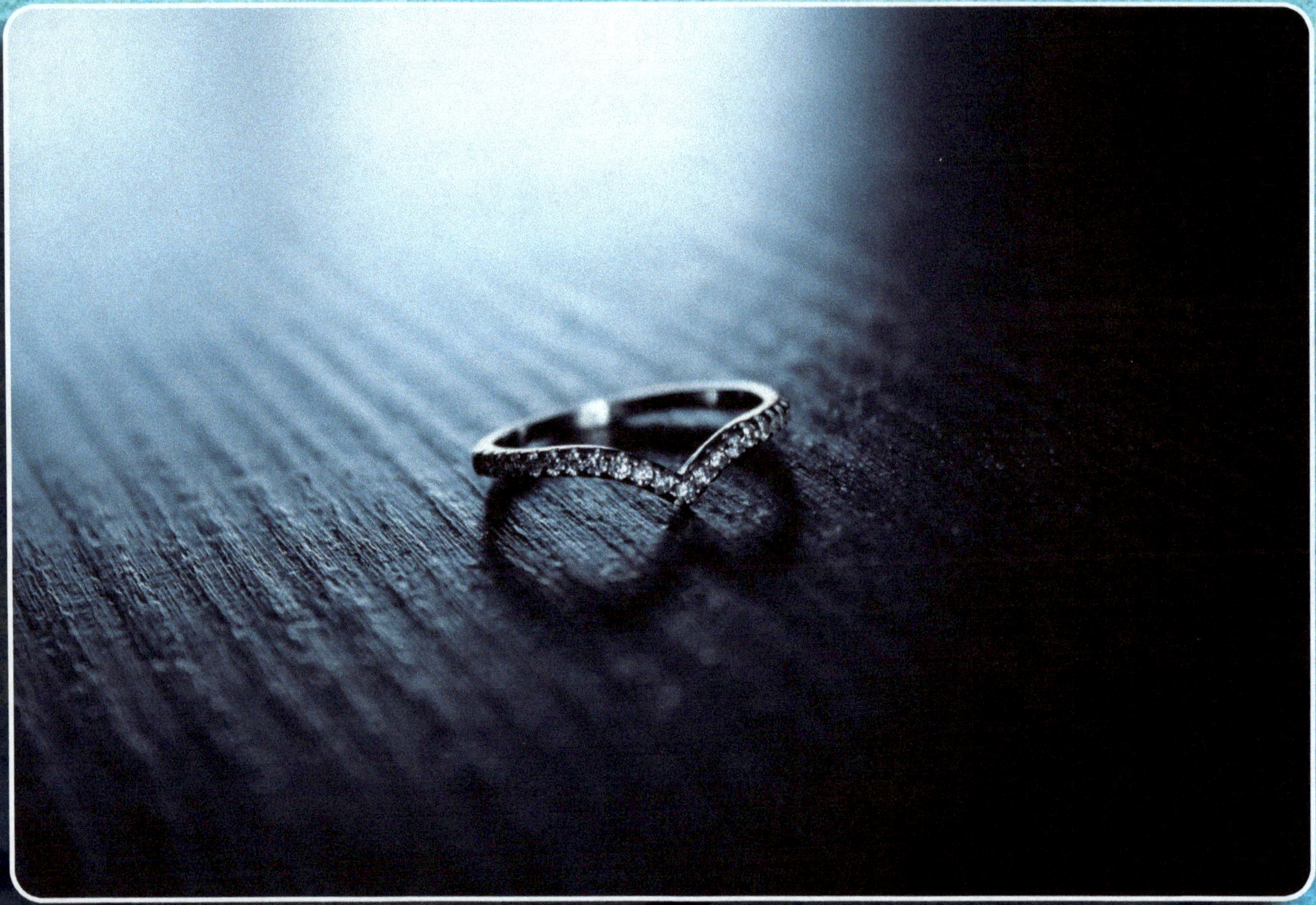

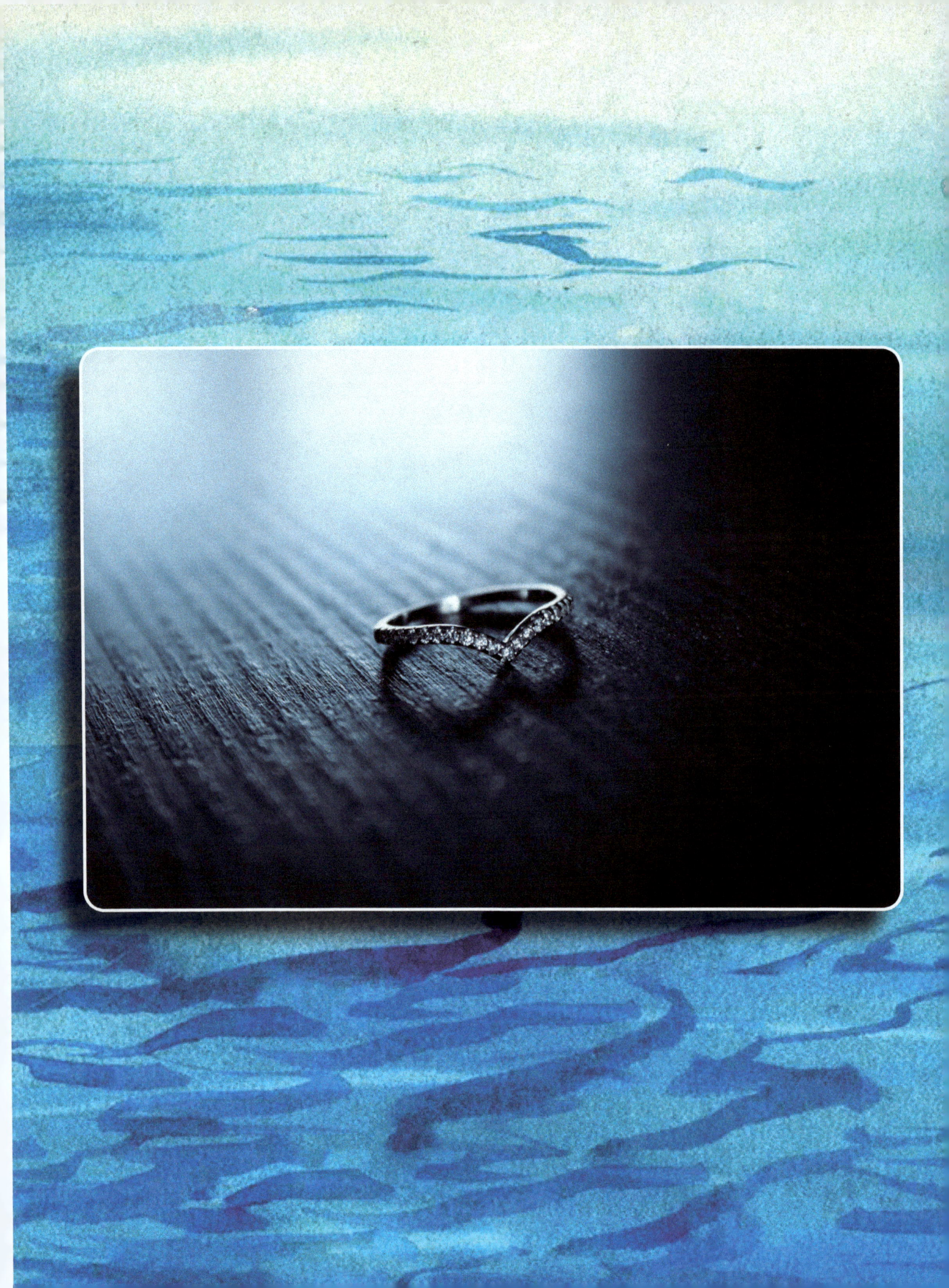

Shadow

As I think
I deeply wonder
How love could touch me
From the deepest blue
To the palest pink
And then I see
The brightest wink
When I look up to you
I see that sparkle in your eye
It's a dream
It's a hope
It's over a mountainside

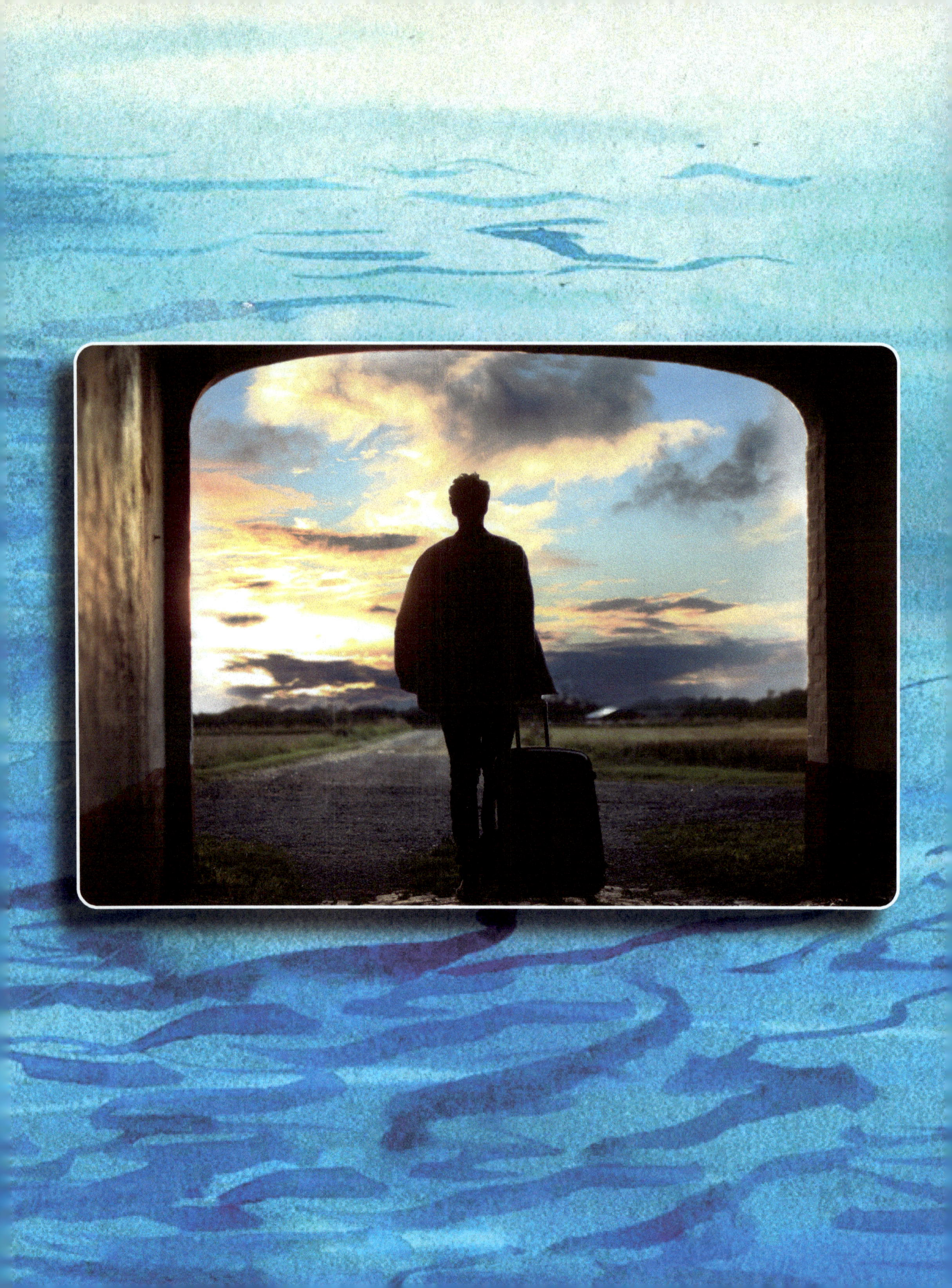

Sunshine

I look at you
As the sun goes down
In the misty air I blow a soft kiss
And you wink, your glamorous smile
Putting that shine in your face
I see your emerald eyes
Your soft lips
That put a smile on my face
As the sun goes down
We hear nothing tonight
But hearts fluttering
Like hummingbirds
As I sit here
My mind starts to think
And I wonder
What I can do

The love I still feel for you
Will never go away
But I know that you don't
Feel the same way

And as I browse
The shadows of love
I see nothing I like
Except the shadow of you
As I look, long eyelashes I see
On those emerald eyes
Looking so perfectly
I daydream about where we could be
And sit and wait impatiently
To the darkness that surrounds me
Overcoming all the light
I wish you were beside me
In the dark and fading night
I believe there's hope for me
A star to wish upon, you see
I'm telling you because it's true
Will you believe my words
If I say them right to you
I wish I could bring all the stars
Down from the sky
And wish upon them all
Maybe then I could have the wish
That's greater than them all

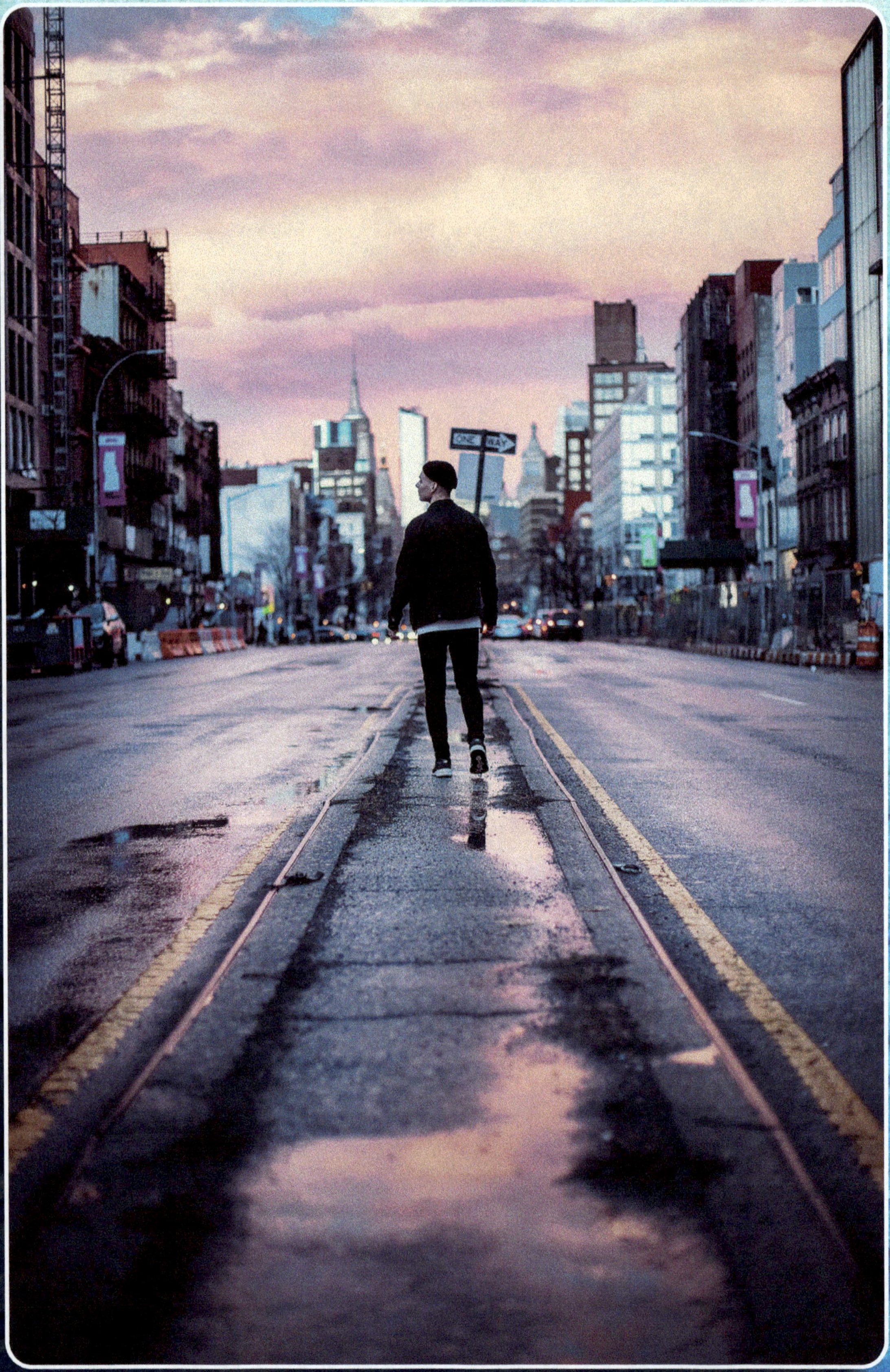
ONE WAY

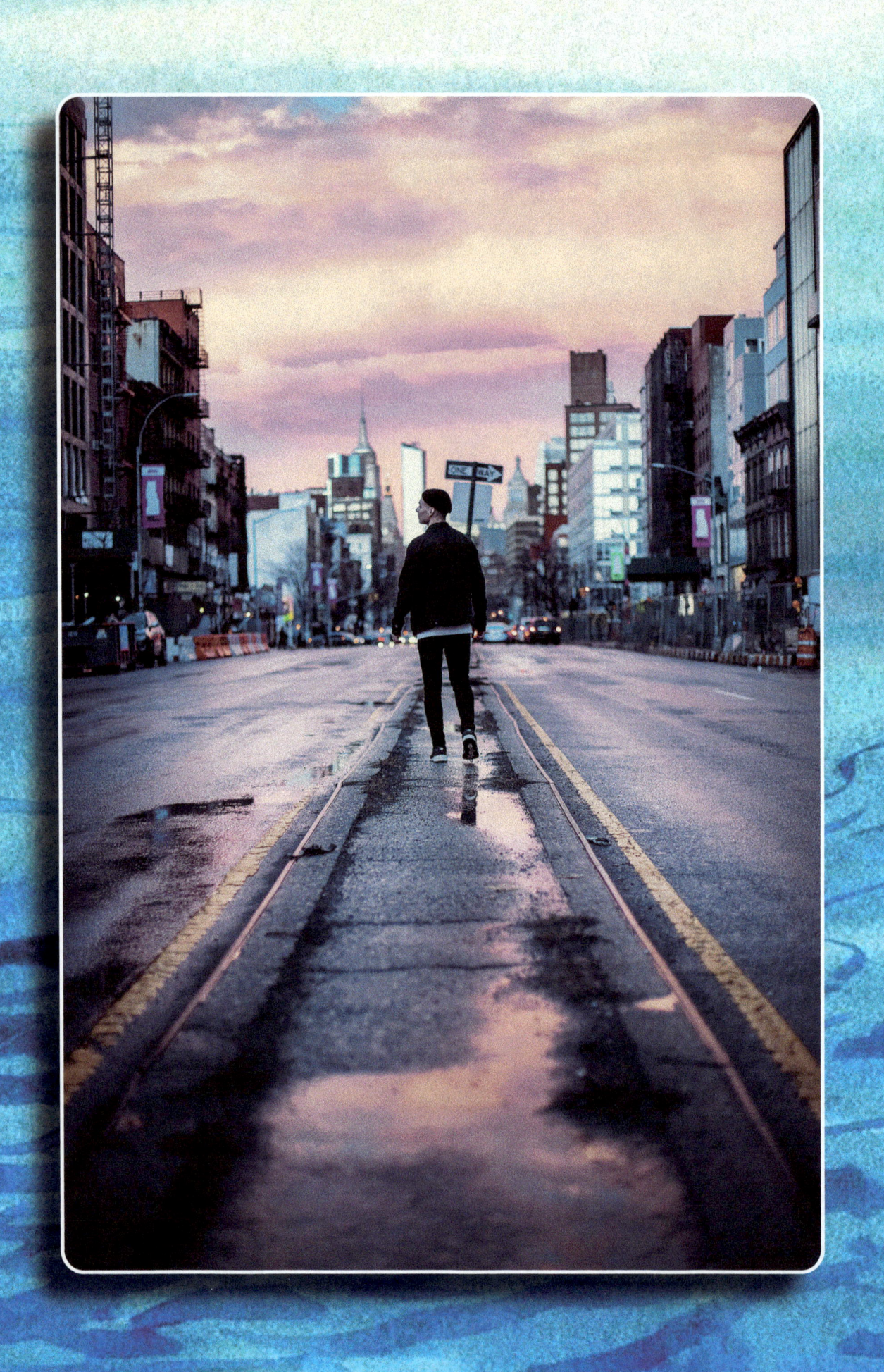

Lost in the Illusion of Love

Words unspoken
Bittersweet things left unsaid
Words I hear from your mouth
That are not even said

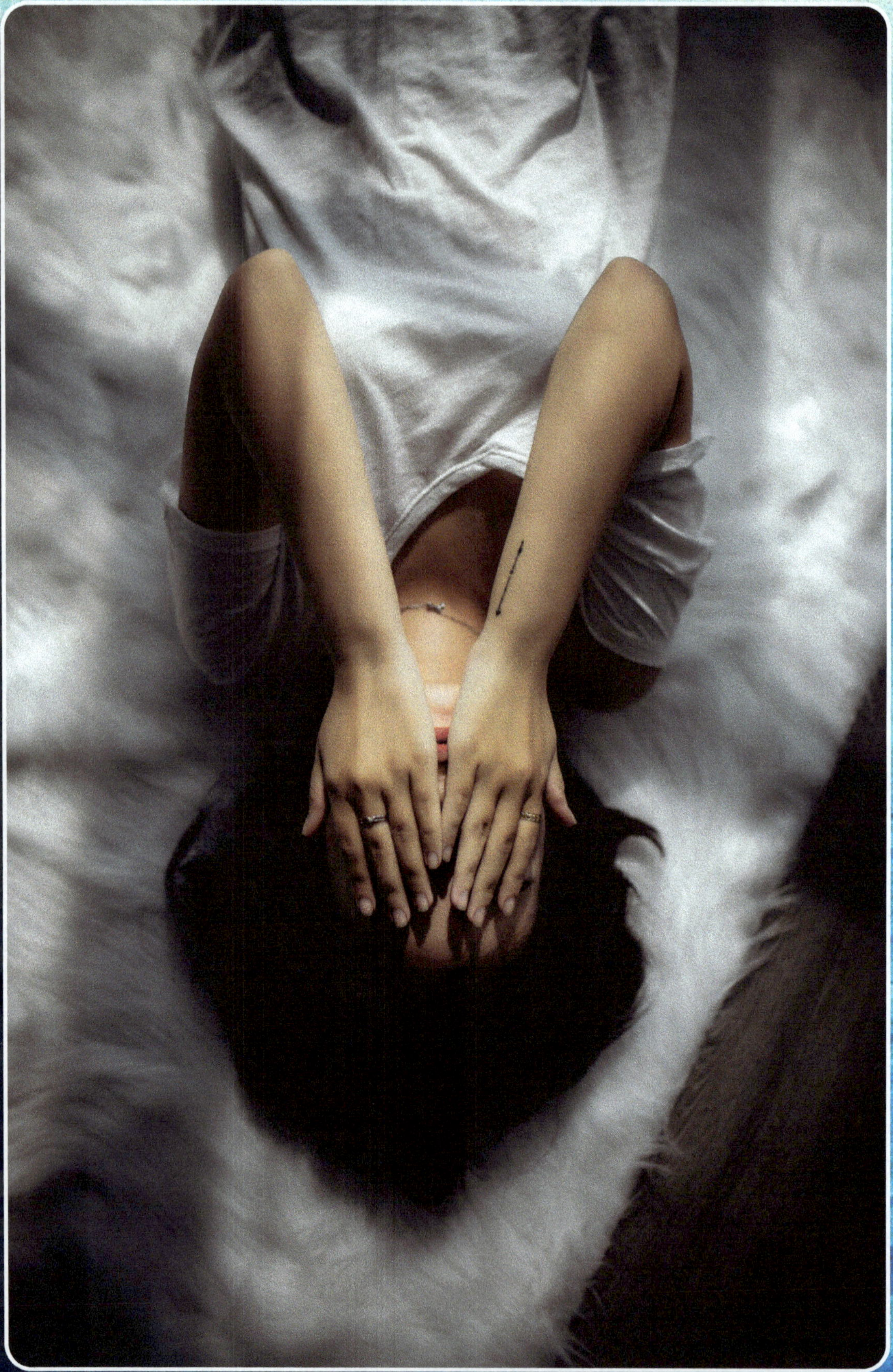

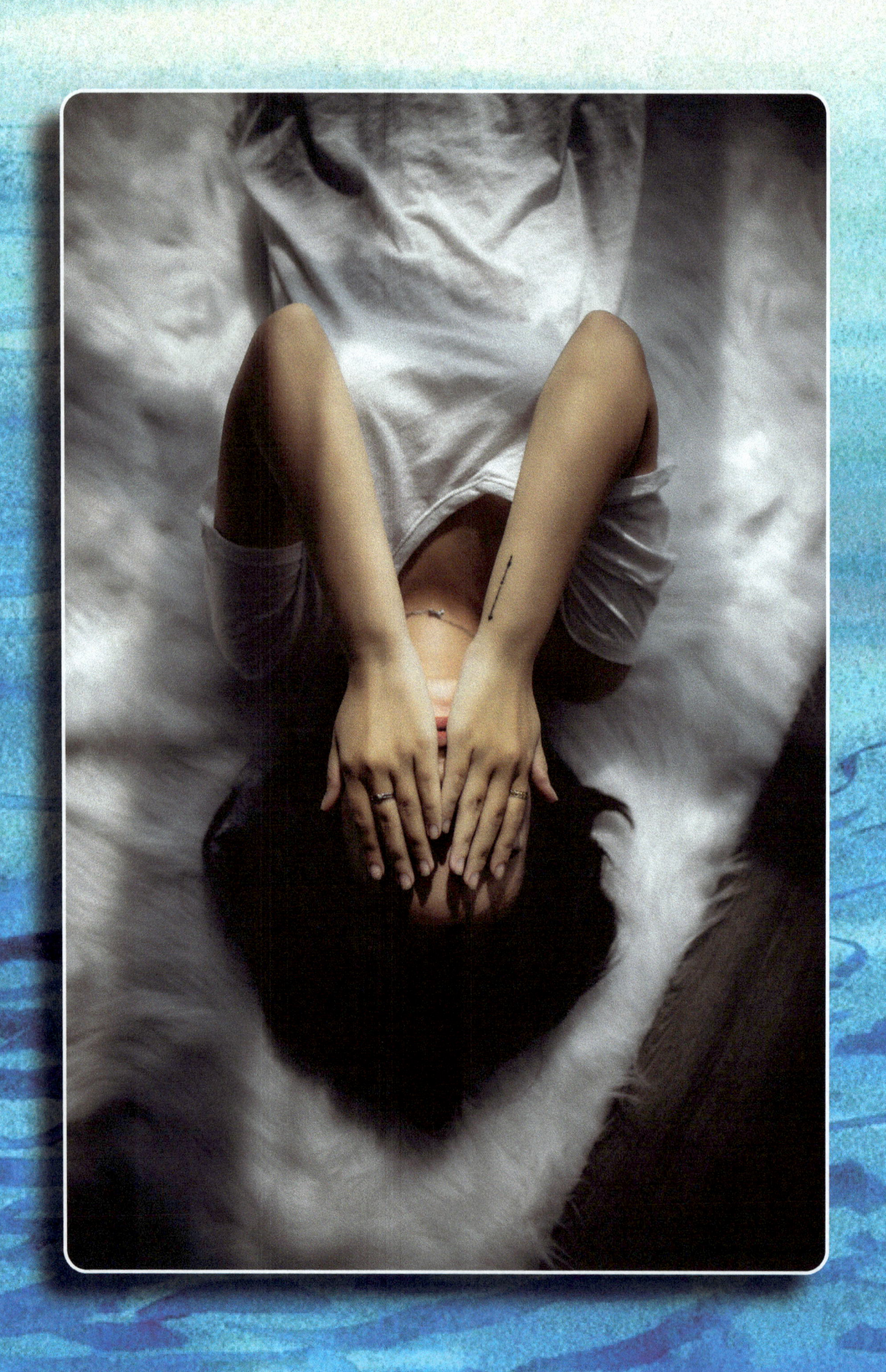

Memories

The memories of you
Are still in my mind
Like the darkest blue
That makes me feel blind
When I think of you
I wonder why
You did what you did
And I try not to cry
I see a broken butterfly
Flying in the wind
It reminds me of a heart
The one I feel within

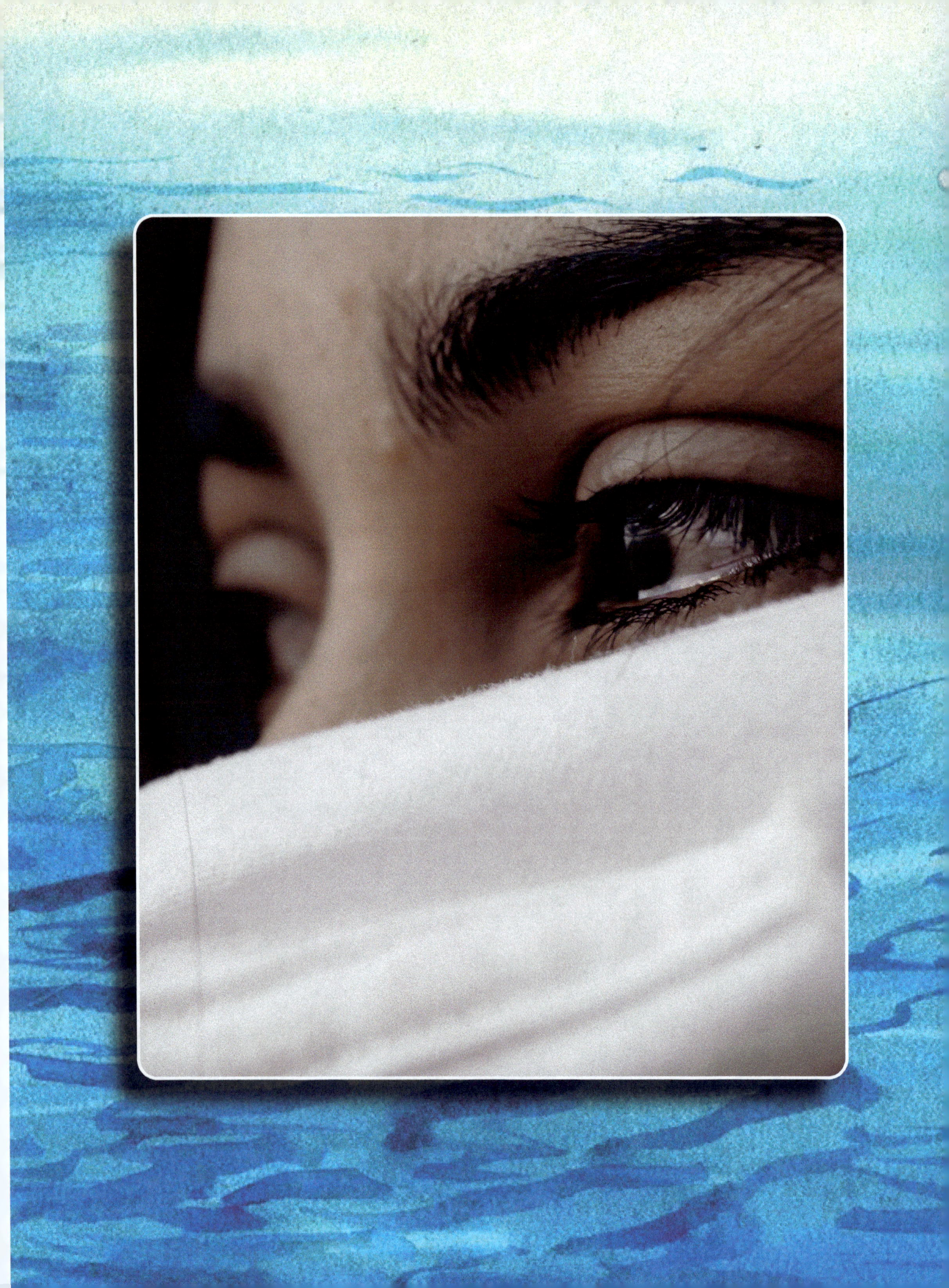

Liquid

A lonely teardrop
Falls to the ground
Without a word
In silence
It crushes all around

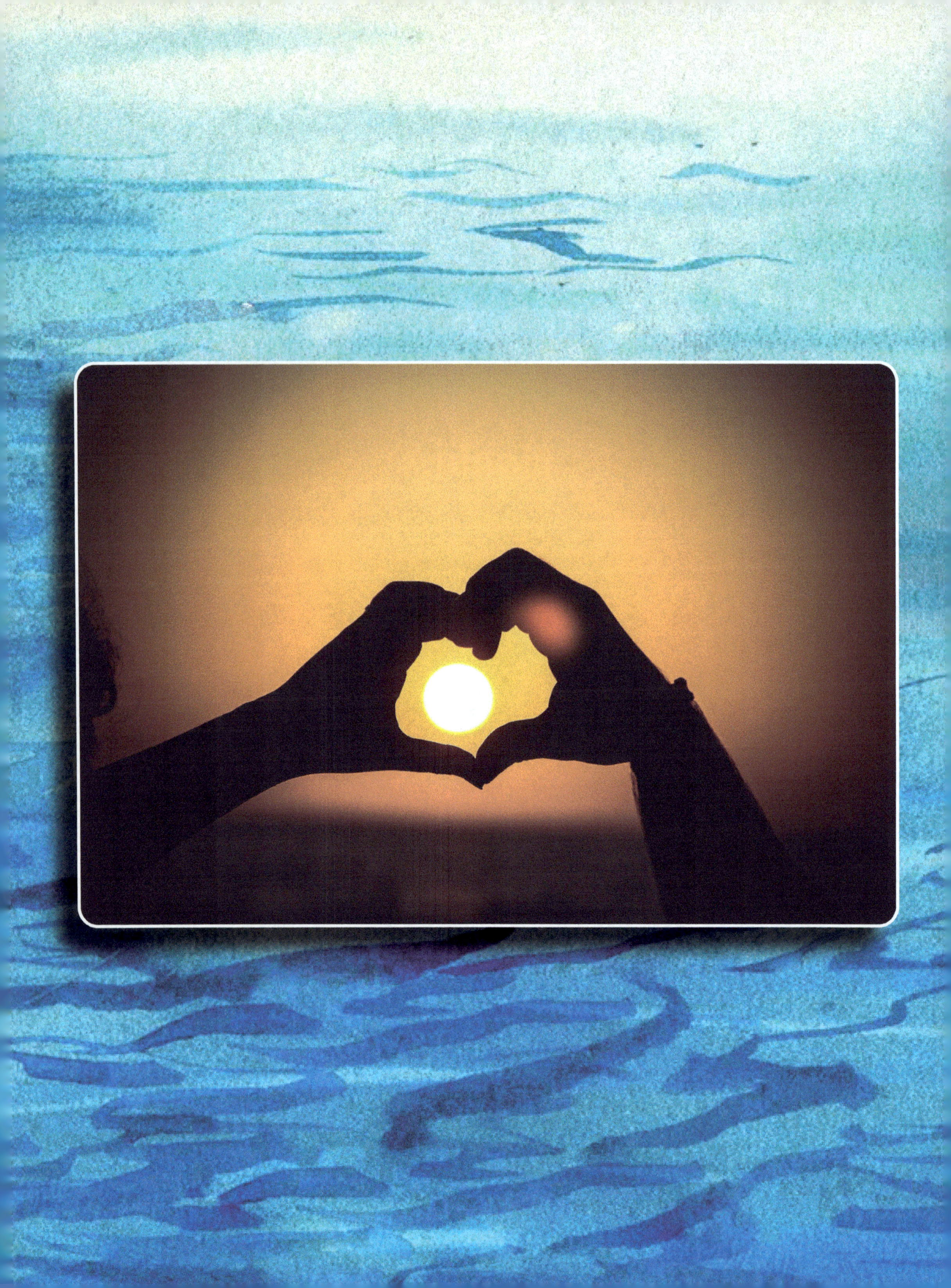

Love

I kept your love
Inside me
Like a dove
That wanted free
Is this life
It all seems like a dream
Everything I do
Everything I've seen
Wish you were here
Wanting you near
To hold my hand
And whisper
Sweet nothings in my ear

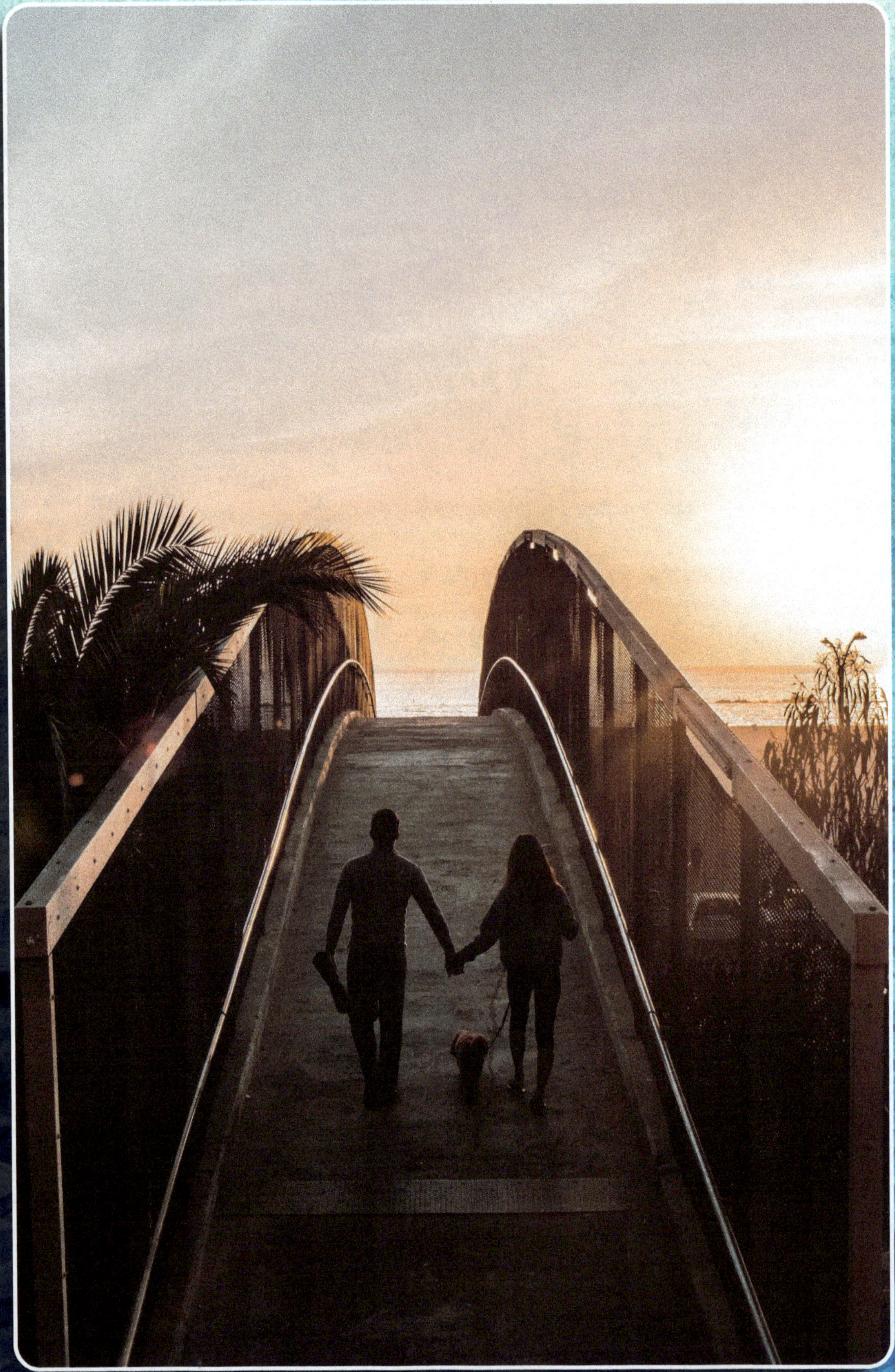

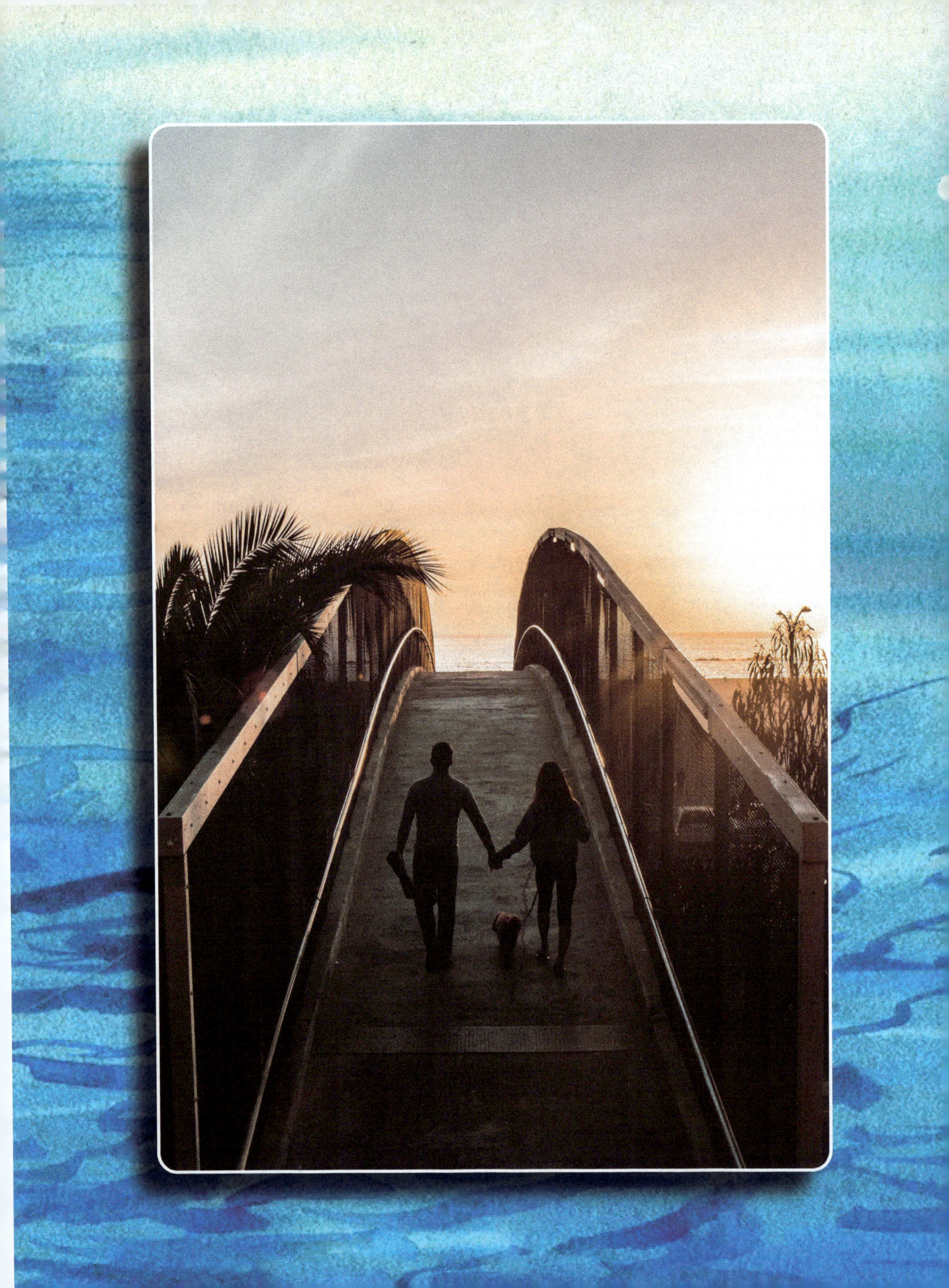

Love

Your love is like a red, red rose
You sense its fragrance
Wherever it goes
If you have it, see it well
Because if you miss it
Only time will tell

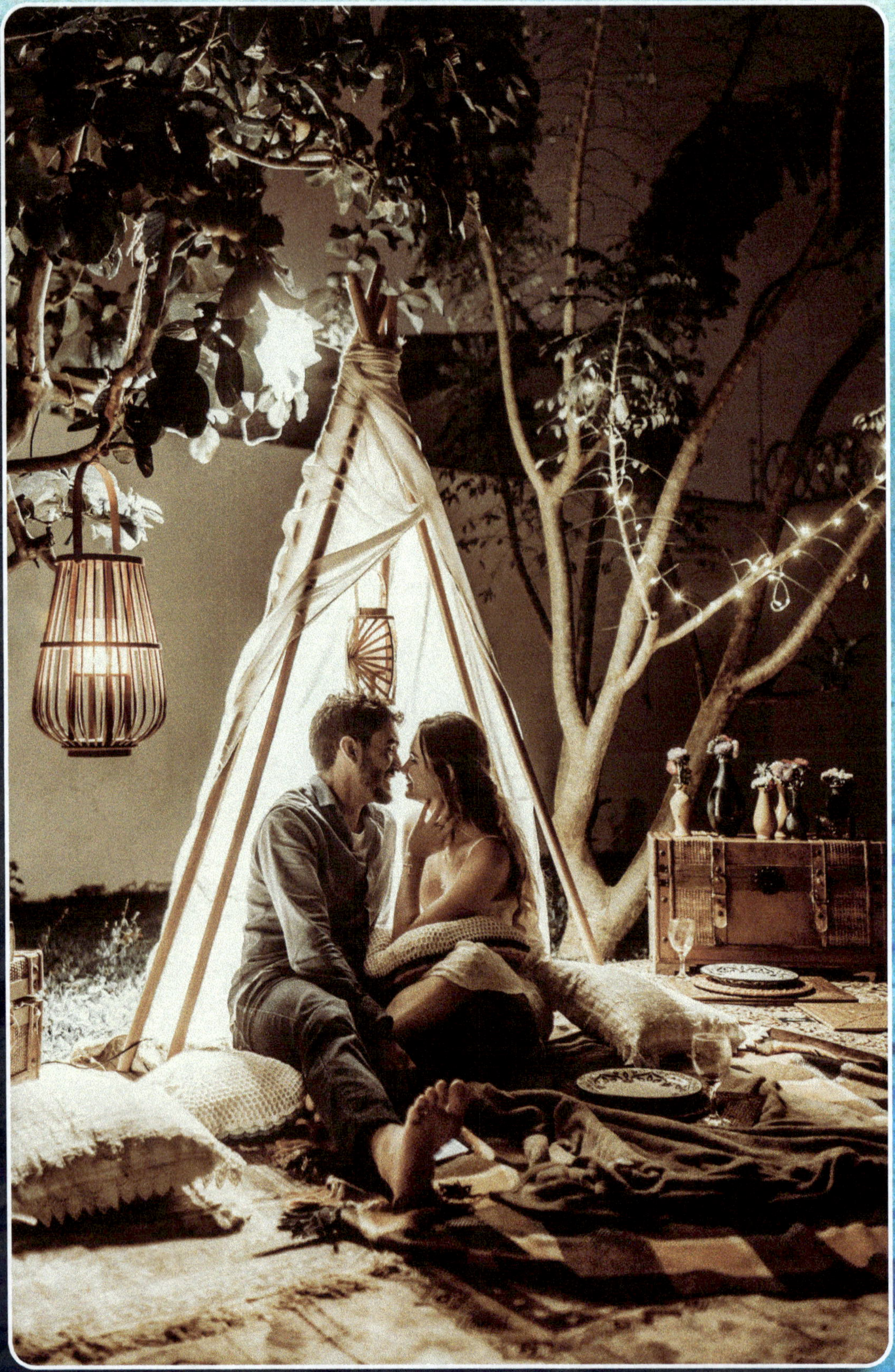

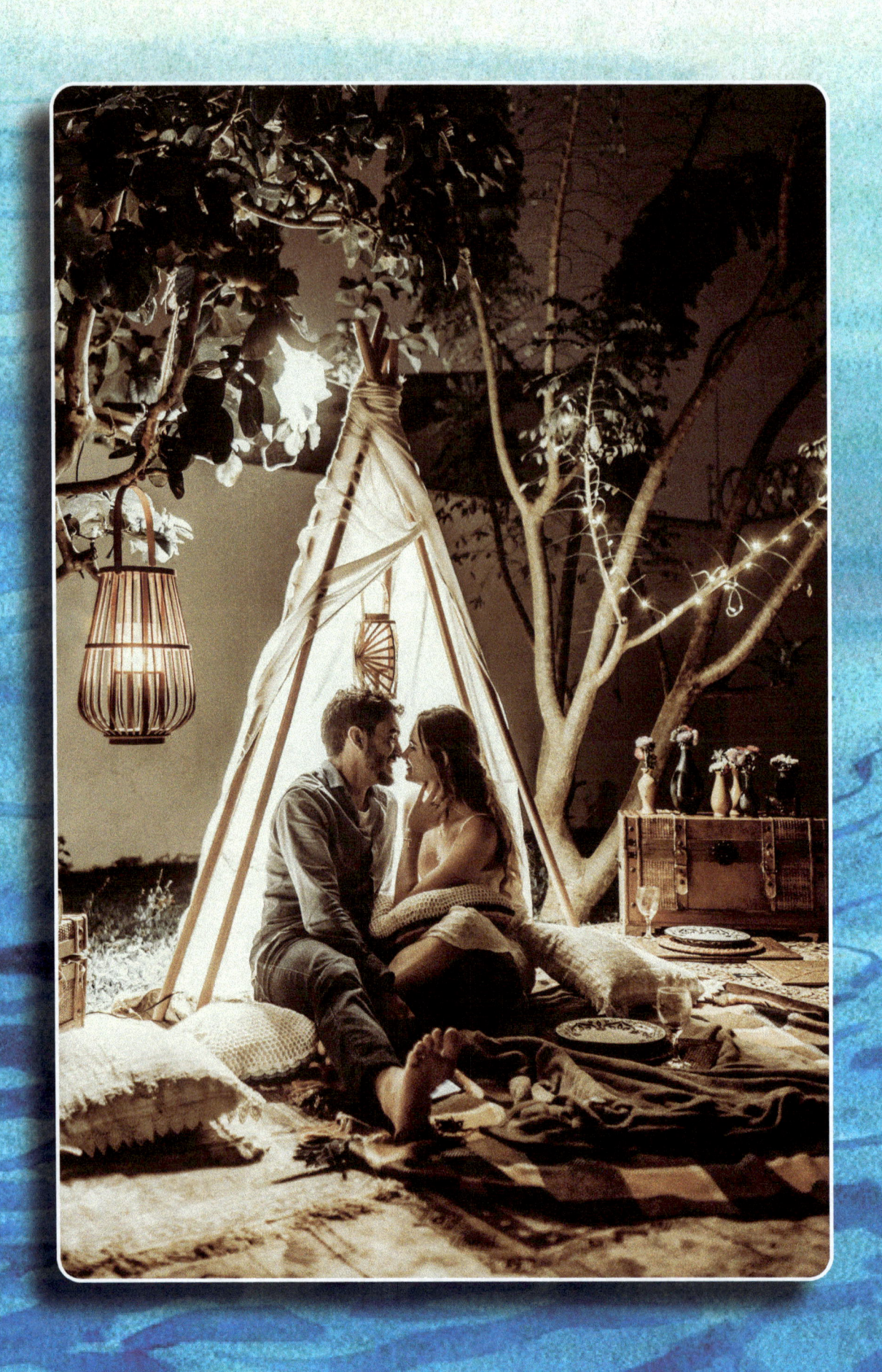

What is Love

Love's a thing with feathers
That perches on our souls
And never does it leave us
Until we both must go
I sit here and think
Of the many problems
That have happened
Through my life
And as I cry
I wonder why
I'm even living
I want to die
Our love is like a long, long river
And yet as delicate as a sliver
It may go on and on forever
But harsh and angry words could sever
Roses are red
Violets are blue
Fires are warm
When I think of you
When I see that sparkle
And the twinkle in your eye
It makes me smile
And feel so good inside
As I walk alone
Along a quiet beach
I hear a voice
Faint, but calling me
I look to the waters
And see a face
A face with dignity
A face that's calling me

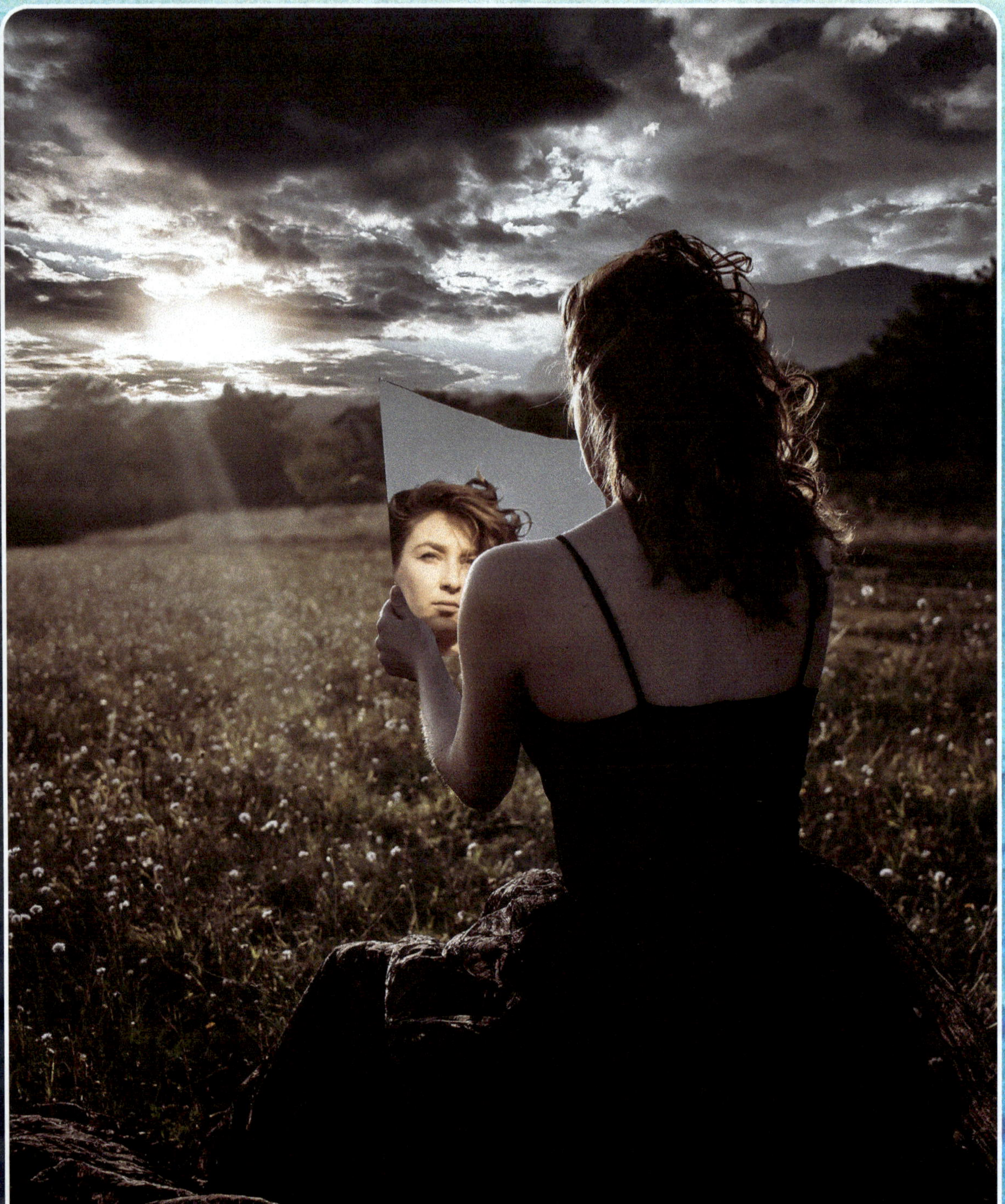

Images

The glimmer
The glamour
The irresistible touch
I feel it in the air
Touching me
Pulling me in
Whispering in my ear
Words
I've been dying to hear

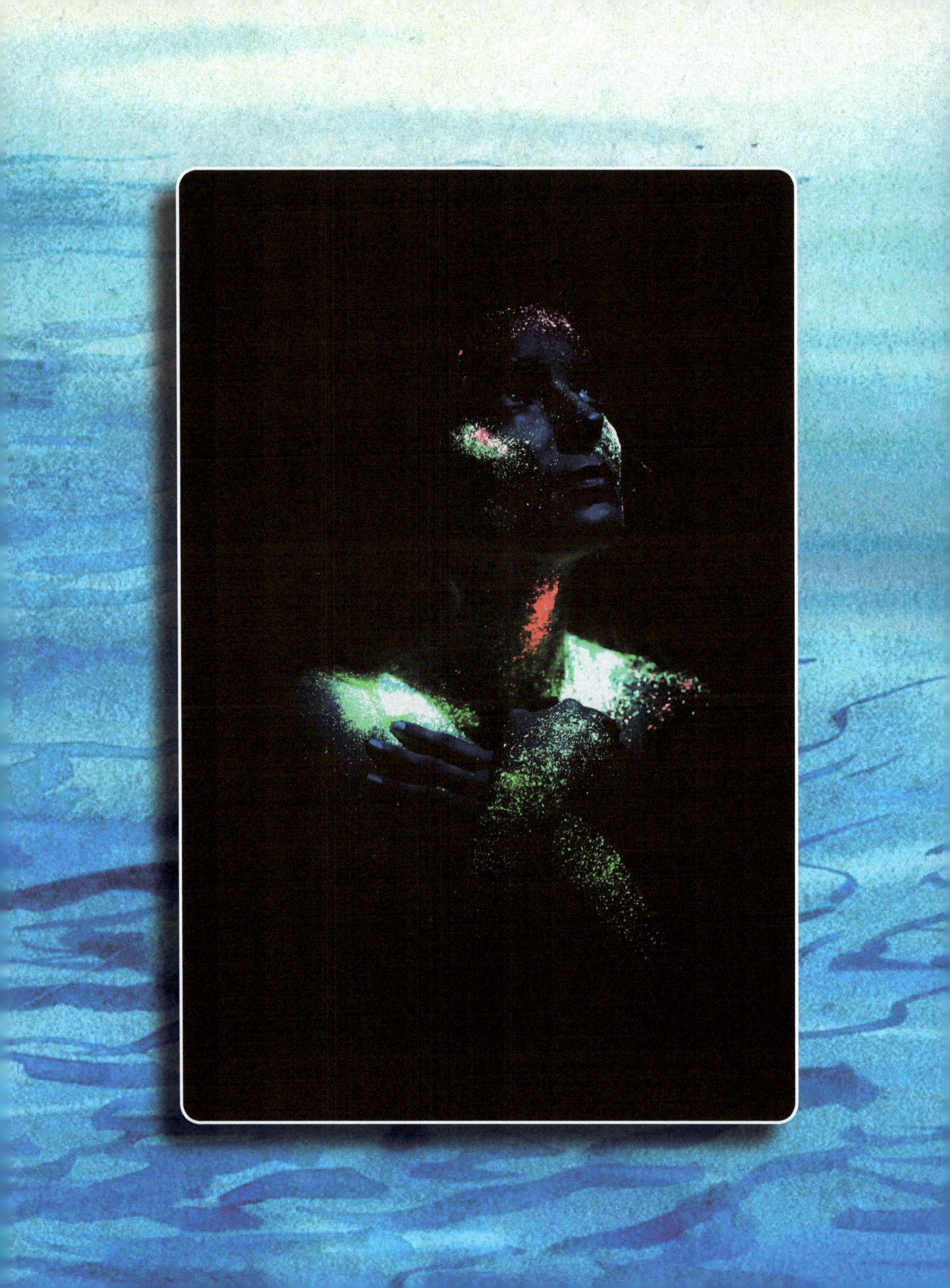

Blindness

To the moon that shines
From the ray within
Fading the sunlight
When darkness begins
I look into your eyes
Deep within your soul
It looks so shallow
Like it needs a place to go
I love the ray of sunlight
That shines within your soul
That purifies the moment I
t's your mystical glow

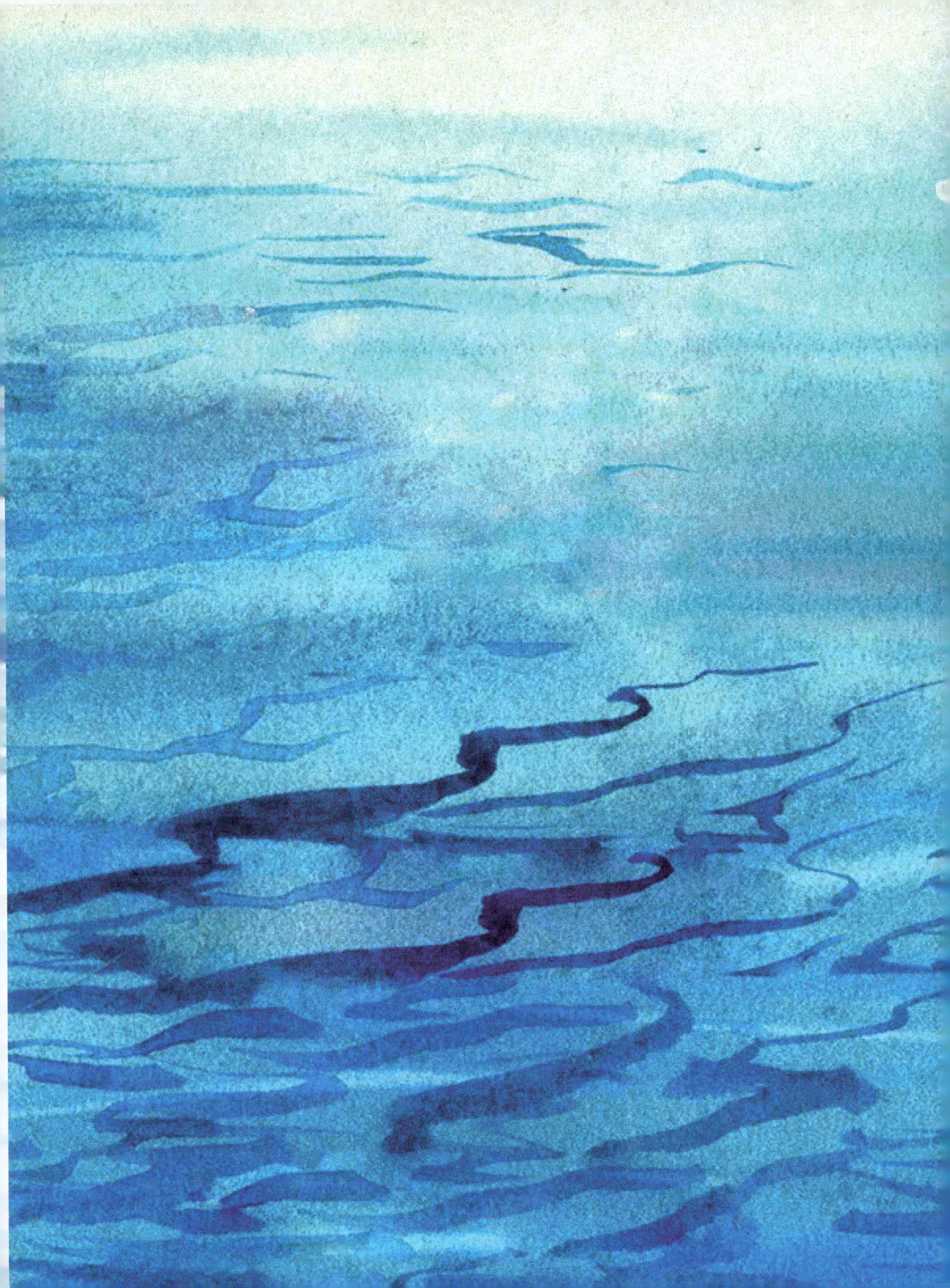

About the Author

Jaime Fidler is a published poet, with two poems in the National Book of Poetry, and this inspired her to carry on writing more poems. Jaime lives on the West Coast of BC in the small community of Aldergrove, along with her two children, who encouraged her to write this book, and two little furry animals. She hopes the words and meaning of her poems will inspire others.

Milton Keynes UK
Ingram Content Group UK Ltd.
UKHW050613041124
450590UK00019B/21